But he got the ball ref!

But he got the ball ref!

Copyright © 1889books 2026. First published in 2018

Cover font: "Belligerent Madness" © 2008 by P.D. Magnus, pmagnus@fecundity.com

ISBN: 978-1-9996440-2-4

www.1889books.co.uk

Introduction

This is a book for football fans, and for those players who want to understand the basic rules.* It is especially for all those fans – we all know them – who love to rant at the referee. Now, there's nothing wrong with that – at least at professional level. After all, when you spend all week being bossed about at work by managers and supervisors who don't know their Arshavin from their Élber, what better way to let out your frustrations at authority without getting the sack? However, if you're going to have a rant, you at least need to know the rules – the current ones, not the 1997 revision or even the Stanley Rous overhaul of 1938 – let's get with it grandad. Certain TV pundits might benefit too! "That wasn't a penalty for me, Ron," (do your job properly). The book is based on the rules at the time of publication. (It doesn't cover sin-bins rules for grassroots level, nor all the ins and outs of elite level VAR – that's a book in itself.)

The book is not intended as a book to teach referees – they can study the rather dry International Football Association Board (IFAB) version or the various guides on interpretation; though junior referees might find it helps make the subject more interesting. Nor is it for rule geeks who want to know what happens if you score an own goal from a corner, the rule on what colour a pitch should be, or what happens if a goal is stopped by a falcon deliberately trained by the opposition to intercept footballs. It will not satisfy aficionados of the obscure; it is not a substitute for *You Are the Ref*.

It would also be nice if certain unnamed managers were to read it and realise that the behaviours they condone or encourage amongst their players are pathetic and juvenile (no, that is not fair to the junior game – which is usually conducted in a far better spirit than the top of the professional game). The game we love has been diminished for a number of years by play-acting, diving, cheating, wasting time and hissy fits of various kinds by managers and players. It spoils it for fans who pay good money to watch football, not a daft carry-on. It has got to stop.

---

*I'm going to use "rules" and "laws" interchangeably, though referees hate them being called rules – they are *laws*, they insist, because laws are open to interpretation.

Law 1 – The Field of Play

In 1863 the size of the pitch was a maximum length of 200 yards and a maximum breadth of 100 yards. In early league football the pitch could be as small as 100 x 50 yards.

Pitches at grass-roots level are a perennial problem. Every time England get dumped out of a World Cup there is the same old inquisition: "How could this have happened?" Why can't we compete at the top level? One of the issues is the appalling state of the pitches we expect kids to play on: too boggy to pass, or the grass not cut due to council cuts, or covered in dog crap. There is too much money spent in the Premier League and not enough at grass roots. The game has been stolen by big money.

In 1999, in exchange for government backing over the right of the Premier League to sell its broadcast rights collectively, the League promised to distribute 5% of its TV income to the grassroots game from 2001 season onwards however, this pledge continues to remain unfulfilled. See @savegrassroots on social media.

And dog walkers: don't let them go on football pitches – or at the very least clear up after them. You may think the sun shines out of your pooch's backside, but slide tackles in what actually comes out of them are not nice.

Law 2 – The Ball

It has to be spherical, between 27 and 28 inches circumference, weigh between 14-16 ounces, and be of the right pressure. Competitions under auspices of FIFA have to carry the FIFA marks:

Balls, such as penny floaters, for back street competitions have to carry some combination of the words "Official" "Super" "Star" "World" and "Cup" in any order.

Footballs have always had the same dimensions. The old pig's bladder leather balls were supposed to be between 13 and 15 ounces at the start of a game – though this was only a requirement of international games – they may well have been, but definitely weren't after a good soaking!

Balls should also carry one of these fairtrade marks.

There is enough money in the game not to rely on child exploitation in stitching footballs.

It is a disgrace that balls with this are like hen's teeth.

Law 3 – The Players

There must be a maximum of 11 on each side, one of whom must be the goalkeeper. The match cannot start or continue if either team has fewer than seven players.

In March 2002 when West Bromwich Albion visited Sheffield United, the game was a most ill-tempered affair, with plenty of history between both players and managers (the jocund Neil Warnock and Gary Megson). On the 65th minute following a high tackle and a scuffle, United were reduced to 8 players, having previously had the keeper sent off. All the subs had been used, so when two players limped off injured they were reduced to 6 players. The 7-player law was then only a guideline, but the referee abandoned the game after 80 minutes with West Brom 3-0 in the lead. The points were later awarded to West Brom. The press dubbed the game "the Battle of Bramall Lane."

Substitutions

Because modern players are a bunch of softies, since 22/23, up to 5 substitutions are allowed (but only "3 opportunities" are allowed – e.g. double, double, single). Prior to the 1965/66 season, no substitutions were allowed and players continued as long as they could stand upright without vomiting. So in that 65/66 season, one substitute was allowed for injuries. But then, certain charming, avuncular, high-principled managers such as Don Revie found themselves having to deal with lots of injuries at around the 70-minute mark – forced reluctantly to bring on a fresh defender when ahead in the game. To save such people from unfair accusations of impropriety, the rule was changed to allow managers of lesser moral-standing the same opportunity of making "tactical substitutions." The number of substitutes then rose to 2 in 1988, to 3 and now 5 for most competitions, but up to 8 in friendlies.

The first ever substitute was Keith Peacock on 21st August 1965 when he came on for Charlton, replacing injured keeper Mike Rose in the 11th minute.

Players who are subbed off should leave the field of play at the nearest boundary line. From 26/27 they will have to leave the field within 10 secs or the substituted player will not be allowed on until the next stoppage. Here's hoping this will end the tedious strolls from the far side and the granny-jogs as they lap up the applause.

The law also covers infringement on the pitch by substitutes or team officials – not something seen in the professional game very often. The principle is that, should this happen, no advantage should be gained by infringement on the pitch.

In the early rules, which player played in goal could be changed during a game "but not more than one player shall act as goalkeeper at the same time." Similarly, in street rules "goalie's wag" is allowed – where any of the outfield players can become the goalkeeper if they get back in time, so long as there is only ever one – in fact the rule is to be encouraged, because who wants to be the kid stuck in between the sticks (or bricks) for the whole game?

Law 4 – The Players' Equipment

This law specifies what must be worn (the right sort of kit, shin-guards etc.) and what must not (jewellery of any sort) – but unfortunately not gloves.

It goes on to state that players must not reveal undergarments that show religious, political or personal slogans or images. (It may come as a surprise *insert name here,* but it's not all about you, you big, arrogant ******.)

Goalkeepers may wear tracksuit bottoms. (Legendary Hungary/Crystal Palace keeper, Gabor Kiraly, was a notable wearer of this item of kit. His preference for roomy, comfortable attire attracting "tracksuit from Matalan" songs wherever he went.)

Studs (for some reason, Americans call these "cleats."). An attempt was made at the inaugural meeting of the IFAB in 1886 to get studs banned. Major Sir Francis Marindin, President of The FA (known to many as "The Majaw") proposed "that no player shall wear any kind of projection on the soles or heels of his boots with the exception of leather bars of an approved pattern." He lost.

Nails were banned except if they were flush with the leather, as were iron plates or gutta percha on the soles of the boots. Leather bars or studs had to project no more than half an inch.

A proper football boot from the late 1800s

A modern football slipper

Law 5 – The Referee

Here's a novelty: decisions made by the referee are to be made according to the laws of the game. But it doesn't end there. They also have to take into account "the spirit of the game." This will be a very strange concept to many managers, players and fans. This is about fairness and respect and not bending the rules or cheating to win. (It is a bit of a shame that all those at FIFA, the custodians of the game, haven't always been held up as true to that spirit – but that's another debate.)

Referees have discretion, but only within the framework of the laws of the game. The decisions of match officials must be respected (by players and team officials). All that crowding round the referee by prima donnas is not allowed. There is not however much in the way of a sanction to stop it – other than a caution for showing a lack of respect for the game, for delaying the restart of the game or for dissent, which are all very woolly and hard to apply in this situation. It is managers who encourage such pathetic behaviour, and it is managers and clubs who should put a stop to it. I would be ashamed to follow many football clubs, the way they go on.

If a referee makes a wrong decision (for example if advised by another match official) they can correct it providing play has not restarted.

Should fans respect the decision of the referee? At grassroots level – always. These people give up their free time, largely for love of the game. So don't be a ****. Even at professional level we should engage brain before criticising; we often have a much better view from the stands than they do, so we will see things they don't and we should appreciate that vantage point. (I'm not even going to mention armchair spectators – i.e.

not fans – they will have untold replays and whatnot to get off on, but have little right to a say. We should never forget that football is a live event for real fans, that just happens to get televised occasionally, not a TV show fabricated for people who wear counterfeit replica shirts but who have never even visited the stadium of "their team.")

But what we see so often is inconsistency – between games and within games, and clearly perverse decisions where the referee must have had a good view. When a referee watches a player judo throw someone to the floor and does nothing, fans have a right to disagree vehemently (check out Roy McArdle's unpunished foul on Stefan Scougall on YouTube and look where the ref was). We need to see the professionalism and training of referees keep up with that of players, and football needs to fund that properly. Only the top Premier League refs earn anything approaching decent money. Others get a few hundred quid a game. You get what you pay for.

The principle that the game should be the same at all levels is important – the debate about video assistant referees (VAR) is an interesting one. Is it here for good? Do fans really want to see it? The danger is that VAR only works on the telly, leaving real fans in the ground angry and confused. At one of the trials when Norwich played Chelsea in the FA Cup in January 2018, there was a lot of hoo-hah about whether Willian from Chelsea dived to get a penalty. He was booked for diving (it certainly was a spectacular dive from a player who sometimes seems to have trouble staying upright) and the ref used VAR to check, but the decision remained. Those scrutinising the video afterwards concluded there was contact made. But is the solution to this not VAR, but that players should not do swan dives on the slightest contact? If there could be a presumption of honesty, rather than a presumption of dishonesty every time, it would be a much better spectacle for all of us. Instead of moaning about whether the tiniest contact was actually made, Antonio Conte would do well to encourage his players not to engage in theatrics. You just need to look at the stats to see there is a cultural problem at certain clubs and with certain players. Perhaps also, retrospective sanctions for blatant cheating and violent contact would help matters, such as fines against clubs and players, or retrospective player bans following some sort of disciplinary process; something going beyond the current retrospective sanctions on players diving.

The referee has a certain discretion over the restart of play: they are required to "supervise and/ or indicate the restart of play" (see the section on free kicks and quickly taken free kicks).

They also have discretion to allow play to continue when there is an offence and the team offended against benefits from an advantage. This so-called "playing the advantage" is inevitably a judgement call and gives lots of scope for questioning the referee's vision and parentage. If the advantage does not follow immediately or within a few seconds they should blow for the offence. It is infuriating when the referee waves an advantage on the edge of the box when the box is subsequently packed with defenders and the ball heads off towards the corner – it is rarely an advantage over a free kick on the edge of the box.

Injuries

When a player is only slightly injured the referee should allow play to continue until the ball is out of play. How many times do we see players sink to the floor to try to slow the game down.

If play is stopped for a "serious injury" the player is supposed to be removed from the field of play for treatment. Only if it is "severe" or follows a yellow or red card should they be allowed to be treated on the pitch, and in the case of a carded offence, only if the assessment or treatment is completed quickly. Feel free to shout "get him off the pitch" (and it does seem mostly a characteristic of the professional *men's* game), or to boo players who drop to the floor like they've been shot, get the trainer on, get treated on the pitch for several minutes, then run round like a whippet on speed once they got what they wanted – a delay and a break in the opposition play. How *severe* was that? Referees will argue they have to err on the side of caution in assessing seriousness, not an easy call when players feign dead. Cheats should be ignored more often. From 26/27 the time a player who has received on-field treatment has to stay off for goes up from 30 to 60 secs once play restarts.

Since a keeper doesn't have to go off if treated on the pitch, we now have the pathetic, modern scourge of keepers going down on 80 minutes to allow for drinks and a tactical team talk. FIFA are likely to review this to try to stop it.

Law 6 – Other Match Officials

There are two assistant referees – or linesmen/women ("liners") to any normal person.

These flag-bearers are supposed to assist the referee with offences when they have a clearer view than the referee. It would be nice if they did their job consistently and didn't appear scared to wave their flags when clear fouls were committed right under their noses. Feel free to berate them when they chicken out of an obvious decision.

Offside

One of the tough calls of a linesman/woman is offside. Every fan thinks they saw it better, and super slo-mo replays expose the errors of decisions made in a split second when they are trying to look at two things at once. This converts all those armchair pundits/sofa subscribers into omniscient foamers at the mouth. Anyone who has ever run a line, at whatever level, must appreciate how tough it is seeing a ball kicked from your peripheral vision whilst watching the last man. It is probably best to give them the benefit of the doubt – unless they are clearly biased and have got it in for your team.

One important job used to be to indicate that the ball has crossed the line, as the "Russian linesman" judged perfectly in 1966, and as the Uruguayan linesman in 2010 so clearly failed to do. Hawkeye technology, now decides, when they remember to switch it on, or whatever. But for the "failure" of the technology in June 2020, and the dishonesty of Aston Villa players, including the keeper, Nyland, who knew the ball had crossed the line, they would have finished on a point less that season and been relegated.

Signals

Signalling for a goal kick

Signalling for a corner kick

Throw in to the team attacking to the left   *Throw in to the team attacking to the right*

Signal for offside. This is followed by one of the signals below to say where on the pitch it occurred

Occurred on the far side of the pitch

Occurred around the middle of the pitch

Occurred on the near side of the pitch

Law 7 – Duration of the Match

A match lasts for two equal halves of 45 minutes, plus a maximum of 15 minutes for half-time. (It used to be ten minutes before 1995.)

A game that many fans play is to guess the time added on at the end of each half (or "allowance for time lost" as it is officially known). The referee should add time for substitutions, assessment and treatment of injured players, time wasting, yellow and red cards, any other cause including significant delays to restart (e.g. goal celebrations) and drinks breaks (for health reasons, and no longer than a minute, when it is blazing hot).

The added time shown by the fourth official at the end of each half is the minimum: stoppages during the added time can be added on, and a penalty kick awarded in added time will run its course.

In a cup match between Bristol City and Brentford in 2000-01, there were 22 minutes of stoppage added on in the first-half after a broken leg, a neck injury (Brentford striker Lloyd Owusu passed out from the pain and an ambulance had to be driven up to the pitch) and a case of concussion. The fourth official had originally held up 13 minutes stoppage time, but one of the injuries occurred after that and the half finally ended after 67 minutes.

Law 8 – Start and Restart of Play

Since 2019, the team that wins the toss can choose to take the kick-off or which goal to attack. Their opponents get the kick-off if ends were chosen or can choose ends if the toss-winners chose to kick off. This takes us back to where it used to be years ago.

The other way to restart play is a dropped ball. This is used where the referee stops play for reasons other than an offence. Dropped balls are no longer contested. The ball is in play when it touches the ground. Since 2019 the rule is that, if play is stopped in a penalty area, or the last touch was in the penalty area, the ball is returned to the defending keeper. Otherwise it is dropped at the point that play stopped for the team who last touched the ball. All other players must remain 4 ½ yards away until it bounces. From 2019 if a team gains advantage from the ball hitting an official, a dropped ball is given.

Thank goodness there is no longer a need for the daft "convention" of returning the ball to a keeper. In the 5th round of the FA Cup in 1999 when Arsenal played Sheffield United. United's keeper Alan Kelly, kicked the ball out of play when David Seaman at the other end signalled a player was down. Play restarted with a throw-in, Kanu, who had just come over from Nigeria, didn't understand the "convention." He picked up the throw back to United's keeper, crossed it to Marc Overmars, who went tearing up the pitch and blasted it in as everyone stood around looking stunned. The goal stood and several United players were booked in the ensuing storm as they refused to play on. Arsene Wenger tried to claim the moral high ground and agreed to a replay after the event – at Highbury again so it was not really such a magnanimous gesture when United were on the verge of a replay anyway, back at Bramall Lane. They could just as easily have chosen to let United score from the restart, but chose not to.

Law 9 – The Ball In and Out of Play

The ball can be out of play in two ways:

When it crosses the goal line or touchline.

Or when play is stopped by the referee.

With the pitch on the left: ball at the top of the picture is still in play; the one at the bottom has just gone out

Law 10 – Determining the Outcome of the Match

A goal is scored when the whole of the ball passes over the goal line between the goalposts and under the crossbar. At kids' football, it seems you sometimes have to remind the players that the aim of the game is to score more goals than the other team. It also seems that some professional managers lose sight of that aim.

When a competition requires a winning team after a drawn match, the ways of resolving it are:
- away goals rule, where away goals count double in the event of a tie
- extra time: two periods of 15 minutes
- kicks from the penalty mark (or a "penalty shoot-out" in common parlance)

There is a long procedure for penalty shootout. Briefly this includes:
- a coin toss to determine which end they are taken (unless ground conditions or safety dictate otherwise – sometimes the police decide!).
- a second coin toss to decide which team goes first – the winner choosing.
- the teams decide the order in which players will take the kicks from the players remaining on the pitch at the final whistle.
- the penalty takers are subject to the same laws as law 14 except that a saved penalty or one that rebounds from the post or crossbar cannot be followed up.
- the winner is the team which gets the best of five kicks. Or, if even at five each, kicks continue until one team has scored a goal more than the other for the same number of kicks: "sudden death" as commentators like to call it.

Law 11 – Offside

Everybody's favourite law. There are two elements to offside; it is important to understand both.

Firstly, the player has to be in an offside position; secondly they have to commit an offside offence. A player is offside when any part of the body other than their hands or arms (i.e. armpit level: see law on handball) is in the opponent's half and nearer to the goal-line than the second last opponent at the moment the ball is played by a teammate. "Played" is now interpreted as their first touch or point of contact; so, I guess if you head it forward then volley it, it is the header that counts.

Just being in an offside position is not an offence. An offence is only created if the player in the offside position becomes active in the play i.e. interfering with play by playing, or attempting to play the ball, or interfering with an opponent (challenging for the ball or affecting the ability of an opponent to play the ball).

There is no exception for a ball that rebounds or deflects off a goalpost, or is deliberately saved by an opponent. So if a player is an offside position and a shot is blocked legally they cannot play the ball. A clear, unintended, deflection off an opponent does not place you onside.

A player cannot be in an offside position from a goal kick or a throw in.

In theory an offside offence can occur in a player's own half – if they were in an offside position and cut back into their own half to challenge for the ball.

Law 12 – Fouls and Misconduct

Direct Free Kick Offences

The offences against an opponent are:
- charging
- jumping at
- kicking or attempting to kick
- pushing
- striking or attempting to strike, including head-butting
- tripping or attempting to trip
- tackling or challenging if considered by a referee to be careless and reckless or using excessive force.
- challenging a keeper who has control of the ball

"But he got the ball ref!" is the common misconception of those still living in the 80s. Back then the offence was just "kicking or trying to kick an opponent" and the referee had to decide whether it was "intentional." An almost impossible job, especially when certain "bite-yer-legs" players would deliberately go "over the ball" to make a point. Whether someone gets the ball first is totally irrelevant! Other species of dinosaur are obsessed with tackles from behind, which was one of the earlier interpretations of the 1990s rule change. It is a tackle from *any* direction which the referee judge to be careless, reckless or using excessive force that is the problem. Just because you were "only going for the ball" does not make it acceptable to threaten to disable an opponent.

Careless means showing a lack of attention or consideration – a direct free kick is given.

Reckless is acting with a disregard to the danger to, or consequences for, an opponent – a yellow card is also given in addition to a direct free kick.

Excessive force is when a player "exceeds the necessary use of force and endangers the safety of an opponent" – a red card *must* be given as well as a direct free kick.

When judging the legitimacy of a tackle the things a referee is supposed to take into account are:
the body actions of the tackler and point of contact: height of challenge/raised studs, the speed of approach, any signs of aggression shown by the tackler (i.e. in a negative sense), position of the tackler, opportunity to play the ball fairly (not just getting to the ball first) and the atmosphere of the game (hostility). All these are the factors were raked over at the High Court in the case of the "most expensive tackle in football history" by Huddersfield's Kevin Gray on Bradford's Gordon Watson in 1997. Gray's negligent two-footed challenge, horrendous to watch on video, broke Watson's leg in two places and led to damages of £909,143.

However, a well-timed tackle is a thing of beauty. It would be terrible for the game if the art were to disappear. All too often we see refs blow for perfectly good tackles, just because they were executed by a journeyman player against a player in front of whom we are all supposed to bow down in order to show due deference to them and their global sponsors. Surely men of such demi-god like status should not be made to fall over by men with feet of clay, even if those clay-like feet just walloped the ball, and did so with precision?

Other offences against an opponent

- Holding – including shirt pulling
- impeding with contact
- spitting at or biting
  all are direct free kick offences.

Other direct free kick offences not against an opponent

Handball. This is an area where lots of fans get confused and embarrass themselves by shouting out. The law keeps changing so it is hard to keep up. This law went a bit crazy a couple of years back but is now more logical again.

The following apply:
1) The ball has to contact below armpit level (see photo).
2) It has to be deliberate, e.g. movement of the hand/arm towards the ball. (This has been the case since 1897, when the rule was changed to stop players kicking it at an opponent's hand to force a penalty. You have had 120 years to understand this simple law – how much longer will it take you to understand. It is a rule that is fair to both sides.)
3) The exception is if you score in your opponents' goal off the handball, whether deliberate or not.
4) Also, whether deliberate or not, if contact is made and the position of hand or arm makes their body unnaturally bigger – this means if your hand or arm position is not as a result of or justified by your movement. There is a judgement call – but if you have your hand or arm in such a position you open yourself to a handball decision.

Handball when below the tape line

The law says if the hand/arm is close to the body and does not make the body unnaturally bigger it won't usually be an offence. Anything other than that, whether that's naturally how your arms dangle or not, risks the whistle.
These changes make a defender's job much harder. In a bored moment try getting a decent jump in without raising your arms or hands above your shoulders – just a ball ricocheting onto your raised arm in a goalmouth mêlée will be enough to give away a pen. The same above the shoulders interpretation also applies in a slide tackle.

A keeper is guilty of handball if they handle it outside their penalty area – it is the position of the ball not their feet that counts.

Indirect Free Kick Offences

1) Playing in a dangerous manner. This is defined as: "any action that, while trying to play the ball, threatens injury to someone (including the player themselves) and includes preventing a nearby opponent from playing the ball for fear of injury. (On the face of it, this is a bit of a weird one. How is playing in a dangerous manner different from using excessive force or being reckless? The rules don't really help. The intention of this is to prevent high kicks that might hit someone in the face, or trying to kick a ball from the goalkeeper's hands.)

Referee's arm raised to denote an indirect free-kick

2) Impeding the progress of an opponent without any contact being made (obstruction). This is defined as moving into an opponent's path to obstruct, block, slow down or force a change of direction when the ball is not within playing distance of the other player. This is not the same as being in an opponent's way – even if that player is a Man United player at home at Old Trafford.

This usually occurs when a player puts the ball past their opponent or nutmegs them and, as they sprint past, the opponent steps in their way. Or, when two players are chasing a ball, one steps across in front of the other. Players will often get free kicks when they run into an opponent looking for a free kick Feel free to boo them and the referee who favours the prima-donna who does this.

A player is allowed to shield the ball out of play if it is within playing distance. This brings us to the "fair charge." Football is not a non-contact sport. A player can shoulder charge a player who is shielding a ball, or to charge when both players are challenging for a ball within playing distance. This charge has to be not reckless, not use excessive force, and not show a lack of consideration. There is nothing about showing insufficient respect for players who cost mega-millions of pounds. Also, feel free to boo players who fall over like they've been hit by a truck at 60 miles an hour, looking for a foul when they're fairly charged, and to boo the referee who falls for it – difficult though their job might be in the circumstances, deciding how much force was used.

3) Dissent, using offensive, insulting or abusive language or gestures or other verbal offences.

4) Preventing the goalkeeper releasing the ball from his hands.

5) There is also "committing an offence not mentioned in the laws." Not sure what this is, but perhaps it should be for wearing Alice bands, or ponytails (in the men's game that is), standing in a ridiculous, poncey pose when taking a free kick or after scoring a goal (no matter how good you are, or think you are – we all know who I mean), or clearing your nose or spitting when the cameras are on you? Also taking scissors to the backs of your socks because your Adonis-like calf muscles are SOOO big.

Various goalkeeper offences:

1) Controlling the ball with the hands for more than 8 seconds before releasing it. The goalkeeper is considered to be in control of the ball when it is between the hands, or between a hand/arm and his body or the ground, holding the ball in an outstretched hand, bouncing it on the ground or throwing it in the air. (A corner is now supposed to be awarded to the opposition if the 8 seconds is exceeded – but most refs can't seem to count to 8 elephants, it seems, or they chicken out.)

2) Touching the ball with the hands after they have released, before it has been touched by another player.

3) Touching the ball with the hands after a deliberate back-pass, or directly from a throw-in by a team-mate.

History. Before 1897, keepers were allowed to handle the ball anywhere in their own half so long as they didn't carry it, which was deemed as taking more than two steps with the ball – they could bounce it but not juggle it. In the 1960s to stop time-wasting by keepers, a rule was introduced that they could only take four steps with the ball in their hands. They tried to get around this by all sort of shenanigans: combinations of steps and dribbling, parrying the ball rather than catching it, and passing it to players and taking a back-pass to allow another four steps and so on. In 1997 the six second rule was added: meaning the ball had to be released in six seconds and taking no more than four steps. It was simplified to just six seconds in 2000, and moved to 8 in 25/26 with the corner (rather than indirect free kick sanction). All this has improved the game, but it is sad that it was needed: that the rule-makers have to play this game of cat and mouse as people try to find new ways of cheating.

Use of sanctions: yellow cards.

The list of yellow card offences includes:

Persistent offending, dissent, failing to respect the required distances on re-start.
Unsporting Behaviour:
- Committing a direct free kick offence in a reckless manner
- Committing an offence which interferes with or stops a promising attack. (Referees to note: the perceived ability or the price-tag on players is not a factor to be taken into account in deciding whether an attack was promising, or the fact that one team is more fashionable than another, or that you are refereeing at Old Trafford.) (See later for discussion on DOGSO – dog what? – just wait)

- Handling the ball in an attempt to score a goal (Maradona 1986, Thierry Henri 2009, Messi 2007, Scholes 2008, Suarez 2010 and other such blatant law-breakers who thereby deserve little respect from proper fans.)
- Showing lack of respect for the game. This has been interpreted as showboating or messing about instead of playing the game.
- Using tricks to get round the no back-pass law. So, if you get down on your hands and knees to head it back, or do a keepy-uppy then head it back.
- Verbally distracting an opponent during play or a restart.

Goal celebrations:

The following should attract yellow cards:
- Climbing onto perimeter fences or approaching spectators in a manner which can cause a security issue – the sort of thing that can put little kids in danger of getting crushed in a surge
- Gesturing in a provocative way (still not forgiven you, Terry Curran)
- Covering the head or face with a mask or similar item (*What? Is this really a thing?*)
- Removing the shirt or covering the head with the shirt

Delaying the start:
- Appearing to take a throw-in but suddenly leaving it to a team-mate
- Delaying leaving the field when substituted
- Excessively delaying a restart
- Kicking or carrying the ball away, or provoking a confrontation by deliberately touching the ball after the referee has stopped play (this seems to happen at nearly every game. Some managers appear to encourage it. Grow up. Stop it.)
- Taking a free kick from the wrong position to force a re-take

Red-cards

A red card is issued for the following:
- Denying the opposition a goal or an obvious goal scoring opportunity by deliberately handling the ball.
- Denying a goal scoring opportunity (DOGSO) to an opponent whose overall movement is towards the offender's goal by an offence punishable by a free kick (but see DOGSO below). This is often misinterpreted as the "last man red card."

- Serious foul play – this is your classic studs raised challenge, or endangering the safety of an opponent.
- Spitting at an opponent or any other person
- Violent conduct. If there is a raised fist, or hand, it has to be a red card unless the force used was negligible. Only the other day I saw a yellow card given for an off the ball incident which knocked a player over. Very bizarre refereeing – someone knocked over using negligible force? Booing was justified.
- Using offensive, insulting or abusive language and/or gestures
- For a second caution/ yellow card
- Throwing the ball or an object using excessive force.

Denying an Obvious Goal-scoring Opportunity (DOGSO)

The rule changed to remove the triple punishment of a penalty, a sending-off and a three-match ban for something which might be just a yellow card had it happened outside the penalty box – such as a badly timed attempt to play the ball, or non-deliberate handball. In this case it is a yellow card and a penalty. If the DOGSO happens outside the box, a red card is shown. All the other cynical fouls inside the box remain red card offences. The factors when considering DOGSO are:
- the distance between the offence and the goal
- general direction of the play
- likelihood of keeping or gaining the ball
- location or number of defenders

It is to be noted that there is no mention of perceived ability of player or how fashionable the club is: this does not affect the obviousness of the goal-scoring opportunity. Referees please note. Naming no names for fear of liability.

Law 13 – Free kicks

A goal can be scored from a direct free kick.
A goal cannot be scored from an indirect free kick – the referee indicates this by raising his/her arm and keeping it raised until another player has touched the ball. If an indirect free kick goes into the goal directly it is a goal kick (or corner if you're hopeless).

Free kicks are generally taken from where the offence took place – although all too often teams of cheaters try to move the ball several yards forward in the hope the referee won't notice, or won't be bothered. Funny how these are usually the same teams who fall over at the slightest contact…

The first exception to taking it from where the offence took place is for indirect free kicks to an attacking team for offences taking place inside their opponents' goal area. In which case the kick is taken from the goal area line. This is rare: it would have to be something like a high kick by a defender or a back pass picked up by the keeper in the goal area.

The second exception is for a free kick to the defending team in their goal area which can be taken from anywhere in that goal area.

10-yard rule

- Players must remain 10 yards from the ball when a kick is taken unless they are on their goal line between the posts. For free kicks taken by a defending team in their own penalty area, their opponents have to be outside the penalty area – the ball is in play once kicked..
- The free kick can be retaken if the 10 yards is encroached upon.
- The person taking the free kick cannot touch it again before it has touched another player.

From 2019 an opponent can no longer join your wall if you have at least 3 players in it. We will never see the likes of Rivelino's goal against the GDR in 1974 where he aimed at Jairzinho who ducked as the ball shot past. *Sigh!* How we tried to replicate that in the park afterwards. "I'll be Rivelino this time. When I count to three: duck!"

The quick free kick

This is a controversial subject. Law 13 only mentions quick free kicks in passing, saying that if a quick free kick is taken then the side awarded the free kick takes the risk of players being less than 10 yards away. Anyone standing in the way deliberately must be cautioned, though: yes, even if they play for a "big club."

UEFA advice to referees is that a free kick may be taken quickly provided that:
- The kick is taken quickly after play stopped (i.e. a few seconds).
- The ball is stationary.
- The free kick requires no management by the referee.
- The referee has not yet started to control the wall or get the opponents back the appropriate distance.

The trouble is that a lot of referees like to strut their stuff, get their spray out, and manage free kicks – especially in a dangerous position. But in doing so and preventing it being taken quickly they often take the advantage away from the attacking team which they are not supposed to do. Some of them create the impression that they think those 1000s of people have turned up to see them. This is not the *insert name of favourite ref here* show. A quick free kick should not be held up for a yellow or red card, if the no-offending team has a clear goal scoring opportunity. They can do the carding at the next stop in play: this is a 2019 addition.

Law 14 – The Penalty Kick

A penalty is awarded for a direct free kick offence (see page 21) occurring inside the penalty area.

Unlike for penalty shoot-outs the ball stays in play once it has been kicked. The kicker can't play it again until another player has touched it, but this means another team mate can follow it up if it rebounds off the woodwork or off the keeper. This does not apply if the penalty occurs right at the death – if at the end of the 90 minutes, and any additional time, a penalty occurs, enough time is added on to take the kick. But the game ends when the ball has stopped moving, goes out of play, or is played by another player other than the defending goalkeeper.

When a kick is taken, the other players have to remain 10 yards away (outside the penalty arc). If the opposition impinge, the kick can be retaken, if it is missed. If the kicker's own team mates impinge and they score it is retaken, if they miss it is an indirect free kick to the opposition.

The kicker is allowed to feint during the run-up but not after they have completed the run-up – if they do they are cautioned and a free kick awarded to the opposition. Goalkeepers have to have a foot in contact with (or behind) the goal line when the kick is taken. Before 1997 keepers used to not be able to move their feet. It then changed to having to stay on their line. They cannot muck about with the crossbar or net, or try to unfairly distract the kick taker, showing disrespect for the opponent or the game.

Law 15 – The Throw In

A throw-in is awarded to opponents of the last player to touch the ball when it goes out of play over the touchline. From 26/27 if a ref suspects time-wasting they can give a visual 5 seconds signal and award it to the opposition if not heeded.

A throw-in has to comply with the following rules, or it is a foul-throw and given to the opposition:
- Face the field of play
- Part of both feet on or behind the line – often foul throws are given in junior football for one foot being off the ground
- Thrown with both hands from behind and over the head (throwing it with one hand and guiding it with the other is not allowed)
- Take the throw from where the ball left the field (Oh, if only they did! This is probably the most stretched rule in football. It is tedious and predictable. A few more foul-throws given for this would soon sort it.)

Opponents must keep at least two yards away from where the throw is taken.

The ball has to be touched by another player before the thrower can touch it again. In October 1998, Dean Saunders scored one of the cheekiest goals in history against Port Vale. Paul Musselwhite, Vale's keeper came out to Saunders at the touchline, putting the ball out of play. As Musselwhite turned to head back, Saunders played it off his back from a quick throw in, then slotted a shot into the empty net.

A goal cannot be scored direct from a throw in. If it goes in it is a goal kick.

Law 16 – The Goal Kick

A goal kick is awarded when the ball passes over the goal-line (other than between the goalposts!) and was last touched by the attacking team.

The ball has to be stationary and kicked from any point within the goal area. From 26/27 if a ref suspects time-wasting they can give a visual 5 seconds signal and award a corner to the opposition if not heeded.

The ball is in play when it is kicked; opponents can enter the penalty area as soon as it is kicked: they don't have to stay outside (but if it is taken quickly, before they can get out, they can't challenge for it). A goal can be scored directly from a goal kick. The kicker can't touch it again until another player has touched it.

Law 17 – The Corner Kick

A corner kick is awarded when the ball passes over the goal-line and was last touched by the defending team. When the kick is taken the ball must be stationary and inside the corner area. Opponents have to be 10 yards away until the ball is played. The kicker can't touch the ball again until someone else has. Short corners are unfortunately not illegal.

Sheffield: the Real Birthplace of the Modern Game

Apologies for the excess of Sheffield references in this book. It is only because they say you should write about what you know. No doubt every fan has examples of oddities they could use to illustrate some of the rules of our favourite game. I'd be happy to receive any examples, or photographs, for any future editions.

While I'm at it with the Sheffield stuff, here's a bit more:

The original Sheffield rules of 1857 were the first to properly apply logic to the words 'foot' and 'ball' and restricted handling and hacking in order to 'civilise' the sport. Designated goalkeepers were a Sheffield invention.
As were:
- corner flags
- corner kicks
- goal kicks from 6 yards of the goal
- indirect free kicks
- the rule that players must not encroach within a set distance of a free-kick
- throw-ins
- tape to limit the height of the goal (this refinement was first suggested by the Sheffield FA) – later replaced by the crossbar.
- change of ends at half time
- forward passes: imagine the game without the attacking play that allowed!
- extra-time
- neutral officials including a referee
- the first use of a whistle by a referee
- shin pads

Though not quite so rules-related, heading the ball was a Sheffield innovation too.

Cambridge is making an audacious bid to claim it was the birthplace of football with its statue of the 1848 rules – a version of the game played by students: "from this very specific patch of English landscape in the heart of Cambridge, the game spread to encompass every corner of the world," they say. This is clearly errant nonsense. These students may have been the first to retain a set of written rules for their version of the early game, but the evidence is that football was being played all around the Sheffield region, and wider, for many years before that. The FA rules of 1863, which were the start of the the codification of the modern game incorporated some of the 1848 Cambridge rules. However, but the Sheffield rules of 1857, probably drawing from the local traditions of the folk game, were arguably much more influential.

Acknowledgements

James Bee, former FIFA assistant referee, Secretary of the Prospect Union of Scottish Football Referees, http://jamesbee.co.uk/

Jack Beaumont for cautioning me, then sending me off.

Megan Wilson – great referee, and excellent flag skills.

Jay and Jane at AFC Unity for granting permission to take photographs – keep up the great work! Also to their opponents, Worsbrough Bridge Athletic.

Hallam FC, and their Chairman, Steve Basford, for letting me take photographs of their game versus Eccleshill United, and to the officials.

Sheffield & Hallamshire County Football Association for the permission on the photos taken at Bramall Lane of the Senior Challenge Cup Final between Penistone Church and Shaw Lane AFC – more entertaining than the FA Cup final!

Rich Wray and his mate for superb acting skills and pretending to shout at the referee for the cover shot.

Tunyi Abongeh for not actually blowing the whistle.

Penalty shoot-out picture on page 19: by Jon Candy (Flickr DSC01678) [CC BY-SA 2.0 (httpscreativecommons.orglicensesby-sa2.0)], via Wikimedia Commons

Picture of tackle on page 21: Pierre-Yves Beaudouin / Wikimedia Commons

Picture of penalty on page 31: (U.S. Air Force photo by Senior Airman Christopher Stoltz)

1889 books

All my books at: www.1889books.co.uk are produced independently – no teams of editors, marketing executives etc. As such I rely entirely on word of mouth to get my books out there. If you liked this book it would be great if you'd write a quick review on Amazon, Goodreads, or whatever sites you use, to let people know about it.

It would be great to hear from you too, if you have any feedback. Contact details are on my website.

Hallam FC

Hallam FC are the second oldest football club in the world, behind Sheffield FC. They have played at Sandygate, on the western outskirts of Sheffield since at least 1859, making it the world's oldest football ground. The football ground is a special place and taking in a game here should be on the bucket-list of every true fan of the beautiful game from whichever part of the world they come. It all started, as football clubs often did, from cricketers who played for Hallam Cricket Club, founded in the second half of the 18th century, who wanted a winter sport (Sandygate is still a dual use ground).

The first ever challenge match took place against Sheffield FC on Boxing Day 1860 at the Sandygate ground. This is believed to be the first ever inter-club game – a fixture that is still played, known as the 'Rules Derby.' Players from the club were instrumental along with those of Sheffield FC in codifying the modern Laws of the game. For example, it was a letter to the FA from Hallam's founder John Charles Shaw which removed "touchdowns" from the Laws of Association Football in 1872.

In 1867 Hallam won the Youdan Cup, named after a local football enthusiast and wealthy entertainments impresario, Thomas Youdan. The competition was the first elimination tournament between clubs in any football code, whilst the trophy is also the oldest Association Football trophy in the world. The original trophy still remains the property of the club and a replica is displayed at Sandygate. Hallam FC play in the Northern Premier League East, the eighth tier of English football, following promotions in the 2020s. https://www.hallamfc.co.uk/

AFC Unity

AFC Unity, now sadly folded, were a socially progressive, alternative women's football club and social enterprise based in Sheffield, providing opportunities for both beginner-level and more experienced footballers. The club's philosophy focused on "bringing the game back to its grass-roots as a uniting force, bringing people together for the love of the game beyond vested interests and the influence of profit – football that has an active role in its community: engaging and empowering women as positive role models, and using the sport to encourage unity, solidarity, and social cohesion."

Started in 2014 they achieved The FA Charter Standard Adult Club status and were awarded the 2015/2016 FA Club Respect Award, took Bronze in Sport England's Satellite Club of the Year Awards and were runners-up in the Most Innovative Organisation category at the Voluntary Action Sheffield *Make a Difference Awards*.

As well as football, they campaigned and raised donations for the Sheffield Food Collective who distribute to the four Sheffield food banks, and developed links with the trades union movement to look at tackling causes of food bank demand such as low pay, and poor working conditions.

Prospect

Prospect is a trade union that represents over 142,000 working people across the UK: professionals, managers, technical experts and craftspeople working in a huge range of industries.

In the sport sector they represent football referees, referee coaches, cricket umpires, grounds staff and administrators. They campaign on pay, terms and conditions, and respect for this traditionally unrepresented sector, negotiating on behalf of members with the likes of the Professional Game Match Officials, a joint body formed by the Premier League, Football Association and Football League. They have been successful in securing holiday pay and pension entitlements for professionals in the Championship and National League. They are working with Women in Football to encourage more women to get involved in football and to challenge discrimination. They work with Show Racism the Red Card to tackle racism through the high profile status of football.

Everyone who is in work needs to be part of a trades union – if you are injured at work, or even outside work, Prospect will stick up for you. The more people who join a union the greater their bargaining strength, and the more they can swing the balance of power back in favour of the employees.   https://www.prospect.org.uk

Sheffield and Hallamshire County FA

The Sheffield & Hallamshire County FA was formed from an 1887 merger of the Sheffield FA (1867) and the Hallamshire FA (1877). It now affiliates over 2,500 teams each season that play in 19 leagues across Sheffield & Hallamshire.

Alongside this, SHCFA registers and supports over 1000 referees, and supports and promotes the development of coaches through FA Level 1, 2 and 3 courses. Its work develops the game by increasing participation and raising standards, ensuring that as many people as possible, from whatever backgrounds, have opportunities to play the game. The junior league is the largest in Europe.

The Sheffield & Hallamshire Senior Cup, which can be traced back to 1876, is the 4th oldest surviving cup competition in the world.

Shaw Lane AFC v Penistone Church FC – SHCFA 2018 Senior Cup

www.ingramcontent.com/pod-product-compliance
Lightning Source LLC
Chambersburg PA
CBHW081504070526
44586CB00019B/2470